Can We Afford A Pastor?

A Step-By-Step Handbook
With Ten Key Indicators
Of Your Church's Ability
To Afford A Full-Time Pastor

Dell Shiell and Diane Shiell

St. Hans

Cover Image: All Saints Church, Lydd, Kent, UK. The oldest section of this church dates to the 5th century. This photo was taken by Diane Shiell during a 2017 home exchange.

For more information about home exchanges—

Visit ChristianHomeExchange.com today.

Printed in The United States of America.

Library of Congress Control Number: 2017917397
ISBN: 0-9631376-5-4
ISBN-13: 978-0-9631376-5-4

We dedicate this book to the congregations we served.
In gratitude, we acknowledge the ministries of:

Bethel Lutheran, Porter, Minnesota

Gloria Dei Lutheran, Cedar Rapids, Iowa

Our Savior Lutheran, Nokomis, Florida

Living Waters Lutheran, North Port, Florida

Table of Contents

Forward

We care about the future of small churches. We have been intimately involved in parish ministry since 1978. For several years, we also worked as church financial consultants.

A lot of leaders in small churches sincerely want to answer the question, "Can we afford a full-time pastor?" So, we wrote this book.

You don't need an advanced degree in accounting or an MBA in church administration to use this book.

Each chapter provides step-by-step instructions so you can evaluate your church's financial position—and your ability to employ a full-time pastor.

Whether or not your congregation can afford a full-time pastor depends on your size (defined by worship attendance) and your finances (defined by debt, budget, what it will cost you to employ a full-time pastor and budget percentages by category). We address these financial indicators in the first five chapters.

Whether or not your congregation can afford a full-time pastor—long-term—depends on your stability (defined by trends in worship attendance and giving, as well as your cash reserves). We address these financial indicators in the last five chapters.

As you "do the numbers" for your congregation, it's our prayer that these ten financial indicators will help you make sound financial decisions with confidence.

Remember—whether you move forward with a full-time pastor, a part-time pastor, a bi-vocational pastor, a retired pastor, a certified lay pastor, a pastor shared with another church, or employing some other creative leadership model—your congregation is the Body of Christ in the world today. Jesus Christ is present. He is leading you.

Remain hopeful. Trust God. Follow Jesus. Rely on the Holy Spirit for the power—the blessings—you need to persevere.

After all, that's who we are and what we do. We belong to God. We work. We trust God. And we persevere, as God gives us the grace to do so.

Chapter 1

Average Worship Attendance

Predicting rain doesn't count. Building Arks does.
—Sherwood White

We grew up when the USA was a *churched culture.*

Diane's parents were charter members of a suburban church established in 1956. When Dell's father was called to become assistant pastor at that church in 1964, there were more than 1,400 children in the Sunday School.

Both of us were born in 1951. In 1966, at age 15, we were confirmed together as part of a confirmation class with 125 15-year-olds. In 2017, the congregation where we were confirmed has a total of nine children under the age of 15! In 2017, the average worship attendance of this church is 160.

Church world in our nation has changed dramatically since the 1950's and 1960's.

Today, though there are more than 300,000 churches in the USA, we no longer live in a *churched culture*. Today, an *aging church* and a *shrinking church* characterize the reality of Sunday morning worship in our society. Today, most Americans don't attend Christian worship services.

Average Worship Attendance is the easiest way to monitor and measure what is happening in churches. The decline in worship attendance is a long-term trend in the USA. This trend is accompanied by reduced financial stability for congregations. Fewer churches can afford to employ a full-time pastor.

When 500 people attend worship every week at a given church, obviously, the average worship attendance for that church is 500. Equally obvious, the financial resources available when the average worship attendance is 500 are significantly greater than when the average worship attendance is 50.

At what point does it become a significant challenge for a congregation to employ a full-time pastor?

We'll let others argue and debate this question.

Our goal isn't analysis and debate. We want to be practical. We want to empower small churches with practical tools by which—*with God's help*—to take charge of their future.

The typical congregation in the USA (60% of all churches) struggles to remain financially viable when it has an average worship attendance of 100 or less—and it chooses to employ a full-time pastor. The struggle is more intense when you realize that 50% of all the churches in the USA have an average worship attendance of 50 or less.

"Can we afford a pastor?" is a very real question with huge impact on the life and ministry of local churches.

You can begin to get a handle on this question, for your church, by getting familiar with your church's average worship attendance.

How To Calculate Average Worship Attendance

1. *Add up the weekly Sunday worship attendance for the year. (Note: We define "average worship attendance" as those in the sanctuary during a weekly—usually Sunday morning—worship service. However, another legitimate definition of "average worship attendance" counts everyone on campus during the worship service—including children in Children's Church or Sunday School and infants in the nursery.)*

2. *Divide this total attendance by the number of Sundays in the year. (Usually, there are 52 Sundays in a year, but there can be 53 Sundays.)*

Example: St. Andrew Church

St. Andrew Church wants to hire a full-time pastor, but their average attendance is 100. Therefore, St. Andrew Church faces a challenge to employ a full-time pastor and still remain financially viable. However, in the following chapters, we will consider other factors that help to indicate a congregation's financial ability to afford a full-time pastor.

Indicator #1. Average Worship Attendance

It will be easier to afford a full-time pastor, if our average worship attendance is 125 or more.

Chapter 2

Debt

There are no problems we cannot solve together,
and very few we can solve by ourselves.
—Lyndon Johnson

Debt is a major factor to consider when asking what you can or cannot afford. This is true for personal finances—and it's no less true for church finances. Debt can put a major strain on church finances.

Through the years, we have seen the full spectrum of opinions about debt held by those who are responsible for church finances. Some of our friends think it's good for a church to have some debt. Other friends think it's bad for a church to have any debt. But, virtually everyone agrees on the need to define what is an *acceptable level of debt*.

For our purposes, it's crucial to identify the level of debt that threatens a church's ability to afford a pastor.

We aren't philosophically opposed to debt for churches. However, it's rare for a church to thrive while ignoring the following three rules regarding debt.

1. *Never,* should debt be more than 200% the annual budget.
2. *Preferably,* debt is no more than 100% the annual budget.
3. *Ideally,* (especially for churches with an average worship attendance of 100 or less) the church has no debt.

No matter what you define as your acceptable level of debt, several dynamics often occur when you exceed that level.

1. People complain.
2. People argue.
3. People leave. (Either by withdrawing their financial support or by removing themselves from worship and fellowship with your congregation.)

Church leaders, please be very clear in your position about church debt—and be united in your convictions. If your debt exceeds what you believe God wants for your church, take appropriate steps to bring this debt within what you have determined is an acceptable level of debt.

The tool most often used to raise a large amount of cash is the capital fund appeal. If your church hasn't had a capital fund appeal in the past five years, it's probably time for such an appeal. A capital fund appeal can help you to reduce or eliminate debt.

When planning a capital fund appeal, you need to establish a timeline and a goal for the appeal. When you set the goal for your appeal, consider taking these two steps:

1. Include plans to support a mission project with a portion of the fund appeal proceeds.
2. If the goal is to pay off debt, a reasonable goal for the appeal is 1.5 times your annual income. This may be given over a three-year period.

Can we afford a pastor?

The second indicator, as you ask this question, focuses on your church debt.

To better appreciate the significance of church debt, we recommend calculating your debt as a percentage of your budget.

How To Calculate Debt As Percentage of Annual Budget

1. *What is the outstanding balance of all church debt?*
2. *What is the church's total annual budget?*
3. *Divide debt by the annual budget.*
4. *Convert the result to percent.*

Example: St. Andrew Church

St. Andrew Church has a mortgage with an outstanding balance of $237,000. The St. Andrew Church annual budget is $158,000.

St. Andrew Church debt ($237,000) divided by its annual budget ($158,000) is 1.5. St. Andrew Church debt is 150% its annual budget.

St. Andrew Church should probably consider a capital fund appeal with a minimum debt reduction goal of $118,500 (thereby cutting their debt in half, reducing it to 75% the annual budget) plus an additional $12,000 for a designated mission project. The total minimum goal of the capital fund appeal would be $130,500. At the end of a three-year period for receiving contributions to the appeal, the outstanding balance of the church mortgage would be reduced to less than 100% the annual budget.

Indicator #2. Debt

It will be easier to afford a pastor, if we have no debt.

Chapter 3

Balanced Budget

*Budget: A record of what the money
should have been spent for.*
                    —Sherwood White

The most fundamental church financial planning tool (other than prayer) is the annual budget. Simply put, the annual budget is an itemized summary of projected income and expenses for a given year. A *balanced budget* refers to a budget in which income is equal to expenses.

Your church's ability to afford a pastor is directly related to your church's ability to operate within a balanced budget. If you are struggling to balance your budget now, how will you cope with inflation? Rising costs are a fact of church life. As every church treasurer knows, if it was hard to balance the budget last year, it's foolish to assume that it will be easier next year.

In the quest for a balanced budget, some church leaders opt for additional debt, selling church property, or spending endowment principal as a substitute for raising income (or reducing expenses) necessary to balance the budget. It's understandable that desperate times call for desperate measures, but these approaches don't generate *income*—as a properly maintained balance sheet clearly indicates. Church loan underwriters are quick to agree that such temporary solutions to a permanent problem are *poor cash management practices*—and such practices normally will disqualify a church loan application submitted to an institutional lender.

Another unfortunate—and from an accounting stewardship perspective, *inappropriate*—solution is the use of *designated funds* (that is, funds designated for purposes other than paying expenses in the budget) so the church can meet its financial obligations. The church should only use designated funds for their designated purposes. When a donor designates the purpose of their gift, it's a best practice to place this gift in a *restricted fund*—and sometimes this is legally imperative (as is the case with most grants from corporations and foundations). Use only *unrestricted funds* to pay for items included in the church's annual budget.

Remember, the annual budget is a spending guide—or a spending plan—that is intended to help you live within your means, while helping you to organize your priorities. It isn't enough to have a plan;

the value of that plan is realized as you implement it, as you follow it.

It's never a good practice to assume that the church is operating within a balanced budget. Churches—like everyone else—must work hard (even under the best of circumstances) to balance their budget. To verify this, your church must maintain—and monitor—accurate financial records.

For a small church, it's usually a real challenge to balance the budget.

Strictly speaking, a balanced budget means that expenses don't exceed income. When it comes to church financials, however, it isn't unusual to hear that the budget is *balanced* or *well managed* so long as income doesn't fall below 95% of actual expenses. But remember, this year's deficit must be offset in next year's budget.

Can we afford a pastor?

The third indicator to help with this question is your budget. Is your church operating with a balanced budget?

How To Calculate A Balanced Budget

1. *Create an income statement (also known as a profit and loss report) for your church's fiscal year. Your income statement subtracts all your expenses from all your income.*
2. *If the bottom line (also known as net income) is zero or positive, then you have a balanced budget.*

Example: St. Andrew Church

The income statement for St. Andrew Church shows that expenses exceeded income, resulting in a net income deficit of $4,200.

St. Andrew Church net income deficit ($4,200) divided by its annual budget ($158,000) indicates St. Andrew Church has a budget deficit of 2.7% (within acceptable levels for a church).

However, this $4,200 deficit for last year is now a line item in this year's budget.

Indicator #3. Balanced Budget

It will be easier to afford a full-time pastor, if we operate with a balanced budget.

Chapter 4

Pastor's Compensation Package

Whether you think you can
or think you can't—you are right.
—*Henry Ford*

How much does it cost to employ a full-time pastor? This is an obvious key component of your budget.

Don't assume the cost to your church for a full-time pastor is limited to salary and housing.

The compensation package for a full-time pastor may include—*but not be limited to*—the following:

- Base salary
- Housing
- Social security offset allowance (usually based on the difference in costs for an employee and a self-employed person— pastors often file taxes as self-employed persons)
- Health insurance
- Life insurance
- Disability insurance

- Retirement contribution
- Continuing education
- Paid vacation
- Paid sabbatical
- Auto reimbursement/allowance
- Salary increases (perhaps 2.8% annual increase)

According to **2016-2017 Compensation Handbook for Church Staff** by Richard R. Hammar, the average compensation package—including benefits—for a full-time *solo pastor* is $65,350.

Here are some additional comparisons provided in this church staff compensation handbook...

The average cost of a full-time *solo pastor* goes up when the pastor has an advanced degree:

- Less than Bachelor: $55,658
- Bachelor: $57,899
- Master: $65,622
- Doctorate: $77,717

The average cost of a full-time *solo pastor* goes up when the pastor has more experience:

- Less than 6 years: $62,773
- 6-10 years: $66,963 (anomaly based on highest cost of benefits for this range)
- 11-15 years: $66,025
- Over 15 years: $67,894

- 8 years: $90,551
- 15 years: $101,766
- 22 years: $113,054

Our point is simply this: you must do your homework when completing a Compensation Package Budget Worksheet. Your church faces its own unique set of circumstances and guidelines. No one can do your homework for you.

Can you afford a full-time pastor?

The fourth financial indicator to consider is the actual cost of employing a full-time pastor. This is of special importance for *churches in transition* (that is, *churches in between pastors*). Make sure that the budget you plan to balance after you hire a new pastor includes all the relevant costs.

How To Calculate The Compensation Package For A Full-time Pastor

1. *Create a budget worksheet for capturing the compensation costs for a full-time pastor. If you belong to a denomination, refer to relevant compensation guidelines as you develop this worksheet. Review the following possible line items for this worksheet to determine what you will include: base salary, housing, health insurance, life insurance, social security offset allowance, disability insurance, retirement, continuing*

17

education, paid vacation, paid sabbatical, auto reimbursement/allowance, and salary increases.

2. *Complete the budget worksheet with dollar amounts you believe that your prospective pastor would deem as realistic.*

3. *Seek counsel and feedback from someone you respect. This may be someone at another church or in the office of your church judicatory.*

4. *Adjust your worksheet as needed.*

5. *Add the bottom line (total cost of the compensation package) to your Annual Budget for a feasibility review of this cost for the budget. Can your budget handle this cost? Can the cost be adjusted so it is affordable and still acceptable to a pastoral candidate?*

Example: St. Andrew Church

The Annual Budget for St. Andrew Church is $158,000. Last year, St. Andrew operated with a $4,200 budget deficit (a 2.7% deficit).

The Pastor's Compensation Package in St. Andrew's annual budget is $78,000. However, the pastor resigned and the church is searching for a new pastor.

After completing their full-time Pastor Compensation

Budget Worksheet, the Finance Team for St. Andrew Church determined that the cost of hiring a newly ordained pastor in their situation is $73,500.

The difference between what they have been paying for a pastor ($78,000) and what a pastor fresh out of seminary would cost ($73,500) is $4,500. This is low enough to offset the budget deficit ($4,200).

Unfortunately, the Pastoral Search Team was informed that no recent seminary graduates are currently available for St. Andrew Church. Several pastor candidates are available but their compensation package is in the range of $77,000 to $82,000.

The Finance Team is looking into options so they can afford a full-time pastor: (1) Do a Capital Fund Appeal to reduce the debt, (2) Find a way to reduce the costs of other staff by using volunteers to do secretarial work and/or provide music leadership for worship.

Indicator #4. Pastor's Compensation Package

It will be easier to afford a full-time pastor if our church can realistically plan to balance a budget based on the minimum guidelines for a full-time pastor.

Chapter 5

Budget Percentages By Category

*Half of knowing what you want is knowing
what you must give up before you get it.*
                    —Sidney Howard

What are appropriate budget percentages for your church?

For financial management purposes, it's helpful to view the church budget as consisting of three categories.

Lump everything in your budget into one of the following three categories:

1. **Building**. Include all expenses related to renting, owning, maintaining, using, and improving the church building and property (debt payment, building and grounds, building insurance, property reserve funds, and utilities.)

2. **Staff**: Include all expenses for personnel, including contracted personnel.

3. **Mission and Ministry**: These expenses

include all the functions of your Mission and Ministry as a church (worship and music, discipleship and education, outreach and missions, fellowship and member care). Include expenses budgeted for your denominational entity.

While every church situation is unique, here are recommended budget percentages for the three categories (plus or minus 5%):

1. Building: 20% *(range of 15% - 25%)*
2. Staff: 50% *(range of 45% - 55 %)*
3. Mission and Ministry: 30% *(range of 25% - 35%)*

When the percentages for any of these budget categories exceeds these ranges, there will be undesirable consequences.

Spend too little on Building—and you are probably delaying necessary maintenance, repairs, replacement or insurance. Spending too much on Building indicates you have more property than you can support.

Spend too little on Staff—and you end up understaffed. Spend too much on Staff and you run the risk of undervaluing church volunteers.

Spend too little on Mission and Ministry—and your donors lose their enthusiasm for supporting a church that seems to be out of sync with its purpose as a church.

In any event, the percentages must total 100%.

Unfortunately, decision-makers tend to treat Mission and Ministry as a primary cost-cutting target when Building and Staff expenses make it hard to balance the church budget.

Can we afford a pastor?

The fifth indicator of your ability to afford a pastor requires a breakdown of the percentage of your budget spent on building, staff, and mission and ministry.

How To Calculate Budget Percentages

1. *Add up Building expenses and divide total Building expenses by the annual budget. Convert the result to percent.*
2. *Add up Staff expenses and divide total Staff expenses by the annual budget. Convert the result to percent.*
3. *Add up Mission and Ministry expenses and divide total Mission and Ministry expenses by the annual budget. Convert the result to percent.*

Example: St. Andrew Church

St. Andrew Church has an annual budget of $158,000.

Their Building expenses are $51,600 (including an annual debt service of $21,600). This is 33% of the annual budget.

Their Staff expenses are $94,800, including a full-time pastor ($78,000), a part-time secretary, and a worship and music leader. This is 60% of the annual budget.

Their Mission and Ministry expenses are $11,600. This is 7% of the annual budget.

The Mission and Ministry category of the budget for St. Andrew Church is woefully underfunded and the Building and Staff categories are overfunded. St. Andrew really needs to reduce its debt. If they don't address their debt, St. Andrew leadership must take steps to reduce Staff expenses. In any event, St. Andrew is likely facing multiple points of stress with respect to church finances and congregational morale.

Indicator #5. Budget Percentages By Category

It will be easier to afford a full-time pastor if our expense categories are within 5% of the following budget percentages: Building (20%), Staff (50%), Mission and Ministry (30%)

Chapter 6

Average Worship Attendance Trend

Change itself is not progress,
but change is the price we pay for progress.
—Clayton G. Orcutt

The facts and figures we have been considering, so far, are helpful indicators about your church's health and vitality on a stand-alone basis.

Average Worship Attendance indicates something of the size, financial resources, and dynamics of a congregation.

Debt indicates an additional level of financial strain for a congregation. *Debt* often makes it hard to achieve a *Balanced Budget*. *Debt* can also skew *Budget Category Percentages* for expenses related to Building, Staff, and Mission and Ministry.

Even when a church has no debt, it's still a good idea to know whether or not the church operates with a *Balanced Budget*, the full cost of the *Pastor's Compensation Package* (especially for a *church in transition*), and to know *Budget Percentages by Category*.

Facts and figures acquire additional meaning when we view them in context. As we look at facts and figures over time, historical patterns and trends surface. This makes it possible to ask about the congregation's long-term financial vitality. Do current patterns and trends suggest that the congregation is stable? Is it growing? Is it declining? What cash reserves does the church have on hand?

The decision to employ a pastor should be made with an awareness of the context of where the church is headed.

For example, what is the *trend* for worship attendance at your church?

Once you begin to track *Average Worship Attendance*, you can compare changes in worship attendance from year to year—you can look for the *trend*.

Let's assume you know the *Average Worship Attendance* for the past five years. Now, you can compare the *Average Worship Attendance* for the most recent year with the *Average Worship Attendance* five years ago. Is it the same? Has it changed? Did it go up or down? How much did it change—up or down?

With the aging membership of most congregations, it is typically a challenge to maintain a stable *Average Worship Attendance* over a five-year period. With this in mind, use 3% as a guideline for evaluating five-year changes in *Average Worship Attendance*.

A church is considered *stable* when the *Average Worship Attendance* fluctuates by less than 3% in five years. Similarly, an increase of 3% indicates worship attendance is *growing* and a decrease of 3% indicates worship attendance is *declining*.

Can we afford a pastor?

Remember to ask this question with your eyes fixed on the long-term situation. You want to know how stable your situation is—long term. The sixth indicator of your ability to afford a pastor is based on your *Average Worship Attendance Trend* for the past five years.

How To Calculate Average Worship Attendance Trend

1. *Calculate the Average Worship Attendance for each of the past five years.*
2. *Determine the difference between Average Worship Attendance for the most recent year and Average Worship Attendance five years ago.*
3. *Divide this number (#2) by the Average Worship Attendance five years ago. Convert the result to percent.*
4. *If there is a change of less than 3% (plus or minus), consider worship attendance as stable.*
5. *If there is an increase of 3% or greater, consider worship attendance as growing.*
6. *If there is a decrease of 3% or greater, consider worship attendance as declining.*

Example: St. Andrew Church

St. Andrew Church has the following *Average Worship Attendance* for the past five years: 100 (most recent year), 103, 104, 106, and 108 (five years ago).

The *Average Worship Attendance* for the most recent year is eight less than the *Average Worship Attendance* five years ago. The only question, now, is if this downward change is more than 3% and therefore worship attendance is *declining*.

Calculation: 8/108 = 0.074

Convert to percent: 0.074 x 100 = 7.4%

Average Worship Attendance for the past five years at St. Andrew Church has gone down more than 3% (7.4%), therefore is *declining*.

Indicator #6. Average Worship Attendance Trend

If will be easier to afford a full-time pastor— *long term*—if our *Average Worship Attendance Trend* for the past five years is positive, flat, or shows less than a 3% decline.

Chapter 7

Giving Units Trend

The measure of success is not whether you have a tough problem to deal with, but whether it is the same problem you had last year.

—John Foster Dulles

The next three chapters will review congregational stability in light of trends involving donors and donations.

First, let's look at the donors as *Giving Units* that provide financial support for the local church.

In the broadest possible sense, a *Giving Unit* is any individual, couple or family that makes a donation.

However, to help us understand congregational stability, we identify *Giving Units* as donors who contribute at least $5.00 a week to support their church.

We want to review changes in the total number of *Giving Units* during the past five years. Let's use 3% as our indicator to evaluate five-year changes in *Giving Units*.

The ministry context appears *stable* when the number of *Giving Units* doesn't fluctuate 3% (plus or minus) in five years. A 3% increase indicates the number of *Giving Units* is *growing* and a 3% decrease indicates the number of *Giving Units* is *declining*.

Can we afford a pastor?

The seventh indicator of your ability to afford a pastor is based on your *Giving Units Trend* for the past five years.

How To Calculate Giving Units Trend

1. *For each of the past five years, identify the total number of Giving Units that contributed at least $5.00 a week.*
2. *Determine the difference between the number of Giving Units for the most recent year and the number of Giving Units five years ago.*
3. *Divide this number (#2) by the number of Giving Units five years ago. Convert the result to percent.*
4. *If there is a change of less than 3% (plus or minus), consider the base of Giving Units as stable.*
5. *If there is an increase of 3% or greater, consider the base of Giving Units as growing.*
6. *If there is a decrease of 3% or greater, consider the base of Giving Units as declining.*

Example: St. Andrew Church

St. Andrew Church has the following number of *Giving Units* for the past five years: 78 (most recent year), 76, 77, 78, and 80 (five years ago).

The number of *Giving Units* for the most recent year is two fewer than the number of *Giving Units* five years ago.

Calculation: 2/80 = 0.025

Convert to percent: 0.025 x 100 = 2.5%

St. Andrew Church's number of *Giving Units* has decreased by less than 3% for the past five years and therefore is *stable*.

Indicator #7. Giving Units Trend

If will be easier to afford a full-time pastor— *long term*—if our *Giving Units Trend* for the past five years is positive, flat, or shows less than a 3% decline.

Chapter 8

Giving Pattern Chart

Great leaders are seldom blindsided. They realize that the punch that knocks them out is seldom the hard one— it's the one they didn't see coming.

—John C. Maxwell

Once you know the *Giving Units Trend* for your church, spend some time identifying your *Giving Pattern Chart*.

The simplest version of the *Giving Pattern Chart* has three columns: Average Weekly Giving Ranges, Number of Giving Units, and Amount Given Annually.

Giving Pattern Chart		
Average Weekly Giving Ranges	**Number of Giving Units**	**Amount Given Annually**

The three-column *Giving Pattern Chart* is simple enough that one can use paper and pencil to tabulate the data from written records of church member contributions and transfer the totals to this chart.

Similar reports produced by church management software are more detailed and complex—and take less time to create.

In the left column, enter the ranges you think would be most helpful in your situation. The most important requirement is that the lowest giving range is $5.00 – 9.99 or something similar. The *Giving Pattern Chart* (like the *Giving Unit Trend* analysis in the previous chapter) only counts *Giving Units* that give an average of $5.00 a week or more.

Once you have a *Giving Pattern Chart* for your church, you can determine how much of your income comes from the 5% of your *Giving Units* in the top giving ranges.

If your congregation is struggling to balance its budget, then it's crucial that you're aware of how much your financial stability depends on a few people. Your church finances could be dramatically affected if any of these few people should die, move away, or experience a dramatic reversal in their personal finances.

With this in mind, it will be easier—long-term— to afford a full-time pastor if you aren't too dependent on the 5% Giving Units in the top giving ranges. This is especially important to monitor if you are already struggling to balance your budget. As a guideline, pay attention if 20% (or more) of your income comes from 5% (or fewer) of your *Giving Units.*

Can we afford a pastor?

The eighth indicator, as you ask this question, is based on your *Giving Pattern Chart* for the past year.

How To Use A Giving Pattern Chart

1. *Create a Giving Pattern Chart for your church with the lowest range for those giving an average weekly gift of $5.00 or more.*
2. *Multiply the total number of Giving Units (column 2) by 5%. Round up to the nearest whole number. This is the number people you want to identify in the top giving ranges of your chart.*
3. *Tally the total amount given by your top 5% Giving Units (calculated in step #2).*
4. *Divide the total amount given by your top 5% Giving Units (calculated in step #3) by the total for column 3. Convert the result to percent.*
5. *If this number (calculated in step #4) is 20% or more and if your church is struggling to balance its budget—you may have a challenge to afford a full-time pastor.*

Example: St. Andrew Church

Below is the *Giving Pattern Chart* for St. Andrew Church.

Giving Pattern Chart For St. Andrew Church		
Column 1 Average Weekly Giving Ranges	**Column 2 Number of Giving Units**	**Column 3 Amount Given Annually**
200.00 +	1	$12,740
100.00 – 199.99	3	$23,400
75.00 – 99.99	5	$17,160
50.00 – 74.99	9	$32,292
30.00 – 49.99	13	$30,160
20.00 – 29.99	13	$17,992
10.00 – 19.99	18	$15,860
5.00 – 9.99	16	$8,060
Total	78	$157,664

Column 2 shows that St. Andrew Church has a total of 78 Giving Units.

Column 3 indicates that the total income received was $157,664.

When you multiply Column 2 total (78) by 5%, the result is 3.9. Round this up to the nearest whole number, four.

Refer to the top of the chart in Column 2 to identify the four *Giving Units* in the highest giving ranges. Refer to Column 3 and add up how much these four *Giving Units* gave and you see that they gave $36,140.

Divide the total amount given by the top four *Giving Units* ($36,140) by the total of Column 3 ($157,664) and the result is .2292 or 22.92%.

Since the total amount given by the top 5% of the *Giving Units* is more than 20% *and* St. Andrew Church had a 2.7% budget deficit, it will be a challenge—in the long term—to afford a full-time pastor.

Indicator #8. Giving Pattern Chart

It will be easier for our church to afford a full-time pastor—*long-term*—if income from the top 5% of our *Giving Units* accounts for no more than 20% of our total donations

Chapter 9

Donor Age and Giving Pattern

The pessimist complains about the wind.
The optimist expects it to change.
The realist adjusts the sails.
          —William Arthur Ward

What do you know about the age of your donors and their giving pattern?

If your congregation is struggling to balance its budget, you need to know how the aging of your congregation will impact the financial stability of your congregation in the future.

Ideally, your church receives over half of all your donations from donors *under the age of 60.* This may seem counter-intuitive because young people have less money and more financial obligations, but older people worry about their money lasting their lifetime plus they are more likely to die.

A simple three-column *Donor Age and Giving Pattern Chart* makes it possible to visualize the level of financial support your church receives from donors based on their ages.

Donor Age and Giving Pattern Chart		
Column 1 Age Range of Donors	Column 2 Contribution Amount	Column 3 % of Total Contribution

As you develop the *Donor Age and Giving Pattern Chart* for your church, include only *Giving Units* that give at least an average weekly offering of $5.00.

With the *Donor Age and Giving Pattern Chart* for your church, you can determine what percentage of your total income comes from donors under the age of 60.

If more than 50% of your income comes from those over the age of 60 *and* you are struggling to balance your budget, it will be a challenge—in the long term—to afford a full-time pastor.

Can we afford a pastor?

The ninth indicator, as you ask this question, looks at the relationship between the age of your donors and their level of financial support for the past year.

How To Use A Donor Age and Giving Pattern Chart

1. *Create a Donor Age and Giving Pattern Chart for your church.*

2. *Add up the Percentage of Total Contribution (Column 3) for all those age 60 and older.*

3. *If the cumulative Percentage of Total Contribution (determined in step #2) for all those age 60 and older is more than 50% and your church is struggling to balance its budget, it will be a challenge—in the long term—to afford a full-time pastor.*

Example: St. Andrew Church

Below is the *Donor Age and Giving Pattern Chart* for St. Andrew Church.

Donor Age and Giving Pattern Chart: St. Andrew Church		
Column 1 Age Range of Donors	Column 2 Contribution Amount	Column 3 % of Total Contribution
80-89	$13,520	8.58%
70-79	$39,052	24.77%
60-69	$49,764	31.56%
50-59	$29,432	18.67%
40-49	$13,936	8.84%
30-39	$8,320	5.28%
20-29	$3,640	2.31%
Total	$157,664	100%

The cumulative total of the Percentage of Total Contribution (Column 3) for all those age 60 and older is 64.91%.

Since the total amount given by those age 60 and older is more than 50% *and* St. Andrew Church is struggling to balance its budget, it will be a challenge—in the long term—to afford a full-time pastor.

Indicator #9. Donor Age and Giving Pattern

It will be easier to afford a full-time pastor —*long term*—if no more than 50% of our income comes from those age 60 and older.

Chapter 10

Cash Reserves

Start doing what is necessary, then do what is possible,
and suddenly you are doing the impossible.
                                        —St. Francis of Assisi

How much money should your church have on hand "for a rainy day"? How much should be in *Cash Reserves*? This is the last of the indicators to consider as your review your congregation's ability to afford a pastor—long-term.

You never know when an unexpected and unavoidable expense will surface. The furnace or air conditioner may "die." Sunday worship services may be cancelled because of a hurricane or a winter snowstorm. Your church needs to be prepared. Your church needs *Cash Reserves.*

Cash Reserves are as important for your church as it is for you to have a personal savings account—and *Cash Reserves* for a church are as hard to achieve. We often feel stuck between what we want to do (save for a rainy day) and what we think we can afford to do. For the typical small church, putting aside money for *Cash Reserves* feels like a luxury.

But, to have *Cash Reserves* is a necessity—and attainable. The key is to take a realistic approach as you set the goal for your *Cash Reserves.*

As you proceed, keep in mind three different purposes for your *Cash Reserves*:

1. **Operational Reserves**. Your initial need is to have adequate *Cash Reserves* to cover possible short-term cash flow issues related to seasonal trends for church income and expenses. Maybe your expenses during the summer months exceed your income. Or perhaps you need to have something set aside for a big insurance premium or local taxes. How much do you think you should have set aside to manage these periodic cash flow challenges?

2. **Contingency Reserves.** Once you have adequate operational reserves, it makes sense to develop contingency reserves. Contingency reserves make it possible to address potential emergency needs resulting from one-time un-budgeted expenses, uninsured losses, or significant loss of income. What is the deductible for your insurance? How much income might you lose if one of your top givers experiences a reversal in their finances resulting in a major drop in their contributions?

3. **Building and Capital Asset Reserves**. The last tier as you build your *Cash Reserves* serves the purpose of acquiring, maintaining, and replacing capital items (buildings, land, furniture, fixtures and equipment) for your church and its ministries. This level in *Cash Reserves* goes beyond the income needs of your church to the *big-ticket items* that usually appear as assets on your balance sheet.

Most churches don't maintain building and capital asset Cash Reserves. They don't schedule replacement or calculate depreciation for capital items. Instead, they take a "wait and see" approach and deal with items when there is a problem. Or they wait until they deem it's time for a Capital Fund Appeal—and address their big-ticket items at that time.

You may choose never to fully develop *Cash Reserves* to cover all three of these needs or purposes. However, we urge you:

**Regard 5% of the annual budget
as the minimum goal
for your church's *Cash Reserves*.**

If your church board wants to build *Cash Reserves* beyond a minimum goal, consider this possible sequence of *Cash Reserves* goals:

1. 5% of annual budget (initial goal for operational reserves)
2. One month of annual expenses (building up operational reserves)
3. Three months of annual expenses (thereby achieving operational reserves goal)
4. Six months of annual expenses (thereby achieving both operational reserves and contingency reserves goals)
5. Maintain *Cash Reserves* equal to six months of annual expenses. Each year, recalculate depreciation for major capital assets and set aside 5%-10% of annual depreciation. An alternative is to develop a basic schedule for setting aside money to replace the roof, the heating and air conditioning, and repave the parking lot (or similar items deemed worthwhile by the Board.)

Can we afford a pastor?

Obviously, the more robust your *Cash Reserves*, the better the chance that your church can afford a full-time pastor. The tenth indicator puts an emphasis on bare minimum *Cash Reserves* equal to 5% of the annual budget.

How To Calculate Operational Cash Reserves To Budget

1. *Determine the monthly equivalent of your Annual Budget: Divide your Annual Budget by 12 months.*

2. *Determine your Unrestricted Cash Reserves (also known as "Net Cash Assets"). Unrestricted Cash Reserves don't include donor-designated funds. They only include funds over which the church has complete spending control.*
3. *Percent calculation: Divide Total Unrestricted Cash Reserves by Annual Budget and convert the result to percent.*
4. *Monthly equivalent calculation: Divide Unrestricted Cash Reserves by one month of your Annual Budget.*

Example: St. Andrew Church

The monthly expense of the Annual Budget for St. Andrew Church is $13,167. This was calculated as: Annual Budget ($158,000) divided by 12 months.

A review of their financial reports indicates that the Unrestricted Cash Reserves for St. Andrew Church is $4,300.

For the percent calculation: Divide the Unrestricted Cash Reserves ($4,300) by the Annual Budget ($158,000). The result is .027 or 2.7%. The Unrestricted Cash Reserves amount to 2.7% of the Annual Budget.

For the monthly equivalent calculation: Divide the Unrestricted Cash Reserves ($4,300) by the monthly budget ($13,167). The result is .33 or 33%. The Unrestricted Cash Reserves equal 1/3 month of the annual budget.

St. Andrew Church should consider these goals for their *Cash Reserves*:

1. The minimum for *Operational Reserves* is 5% ($7,900) of the Annual Budget ($158,000). The church's current *Cash Reserves* are $4,300 (2.7% of the Annual Budget). An additional 2.3% ($3,600) is needed to reach desired minimum *Cash Reserves* (5%).
2. After reaching the 5% minimum *Cash Reserves,* the church should consider advancing their *Cash Reserves* toward the target of one-month of expenses—*if, and only if,* the Board wants this.

Indicator #10. Cash Reserves

It will be easier to afford a full-time pastor— *long-term*—if our *Cash Reserves* are more than 5% of our Annual Budget.

Chapter 11

Conclusion

The best time to plant a tree is twenty years ago,
the second best time is now.
—Anonymous

We know that Christianity isn't all about money and the church isn't a business. Still, we believe it isn't a coincidence that nearly half of Jesus' parables deal with money. Jesus talked more about money and possessions than any other subject except for the kingdom of God.

For Christians, money is never an end in and of itself. Money is always a means to an end. We, also, believe that what is important about money is our stewardship of it. This conviction underlies all the effort that went into writing this book.

Having said this, where do you go from here?

Did you only read this book? Or did you *do the numbers*, too?

If you haven't yet completed the exercise of applying the calculations for each of the *Ten Indicators* to your own situation, then, that should be your first "next step."

We have listed the *Ten Indicators* in the order that we think makes the most sense.

One of the messages we hope to communicate is that—when it comes to the ability to afford a full-time pastor—church size matters. The best measure of church size is average worship attendance. Most struggling churches need to know this. You need to know that if your congregation has an average worship attendance of 100 or less, it's not a slam-dunk for you to afford a full-time pastor. Church size isn't the only factor, but it's the crucial starting-point as you get serious about asking, "Can we afford a pastor?"

Church debt is the obvious second indicator. If your church is small—and you have debt—don't let the fact that you're struggling financially be a surprise. We want you to see a path so you can take charge of your situation. You're not a victim! It's a challenge to be small. It's imprudent to be small—and carry debt. We want you to consider debt before we bring up the importance of a balanced budget for an obvious reason. Debt is the number one obstacle to a balanced budget. A small church has a much better chance of balancing its budget when debt is under control. Still, reducing or eliminating debt is no guarantee that your budget is under control. You need to be honest and realistic about your budget. Is it really a balanced budget? Are you paying your bills with income—or are you spending something other than income too? Debt? Endowment principal? Proceeds from the sale of property?

For the typical small church, the cost of a full-time pastor is its number one expense. The reality of our times—with our *aging churches* and *shrinking churches*—means that many small churches formerly were not small churches. Formerly, these churches employed full-time pastors. It's hard to know—and harder still to accept—when this is no longer possible. The only way to figure this out is to make sure that your proposed balanced budget is based on the actual cost of a compensation package for a pastor. Small *churches in transition* (that is, *churches in between pastors*) have the unique opportunity to review the impact of the cost of a full-time pastor on their ability to balance their budget.

The next indicator—budget percentages by category—urges church leaders to review the impact of building and staff expenses on their mission and ministry. You need guidelines as you make tough choices. If building expenses or staff expenses are unbalanced (in light of recommended guidelines), how are you going to restore balance?

We are convinced that if you *do the numbers* for the first five indicators—and include others in a discussion about the results—you will see decisions you need to make and actions you can take to strengthen your church. Consensus about the answer to the question, "Can we afford a pastor," will become increasingly clear.

The remaining five indicators, likewise, urge your leadership onward to increasingly advanced levels of skill in taking charge of your church's finances.

This may be hard for you to hear, but the goal isn't to have a full-time pastor. The goal is to be faithful as the church. Faithfulness requires honesty. Faithfulness also requires the humility to let God guide you as you decide what kind of pastoral leadership is appropriate for your church— full-time pastor, part-time pastor, bi-vocational pastor, retired pastor, certified lay pastor, pastor shared with another church, or employing some other creative leadership model.

Several times we have referred to the changing times that are giving rise to so many struggling churches. This time of change is still a good time to be the church. We need to trust that God is God—and that our lives and our churches are in God's hands. We have an awesome mission as the church of Jesus Christ! Keep your focus on that mission—and we are confident that you will put this handbook to good use.

In closing, we want to share a quote from our book, **Go, Pastor. Go!**

We in the church are slowly waking up to the reality of change. Elizabeth Eaton, Presiding Bishop of the Evangelical Lutheran Church in America (ELCA), acknowledges, "We are in the middle of a seismic shift in the church." Change is here to stay. Now, what can we do about it?

APPENDIX

Ten Indicators To Help You Review
Your Church's Ability
To Afford A Full-Time Pastor

INDICATOR	It will be easier to afford a full-time pastor, if...
#1. Average Worship Attendance	... our *Average Worship Attendance* is 125 or more.
#2. Debt	... we have no *Debt.*
#3. Balanced Budget	... we operate with a *Balanced Budget.*
#4. Pastor's Compensation Package	... our church can realistically plan to balance a budget based on the minimum guidelines for a full-time pastor.
#5. Budget Percentages By Category	... our expense categories are within 5% of the following budget percentages: Building (20%), Staff (50%), Mission and Ministry 30%.

INDICATOR	It will be easier to afford a full-time pastor, if...
#6. Average Worship Attendance Trend	... our *Average Worship Attendance Trend* for the past five years is positive, flat, or shows less than a 3% decline.
#7. Giving Units Trend	... our *Giving Units Trend* for the past five years is positive, flat, or shows less than a 3% decline.
#8. Giving Pattern Chart	... income from the top 5% of our *Giving Units* accounts for no more than 20% of our total donations.
#9. Donor Age and Giving Pattern	... no more than 50% of our income comes from those age 60 and older.
#10. Cash Reserves	... our *Cash Reserves* are more than 5% of our Annual Budget.

COMIC RELIEF

We Christians have a hard time laughing—at ourselves, at life, at the situation that faces us. So, we share the following ditty about *dead horses* for the sake of comic relief. It would be a mistake to imagine we are implying that small churches are dead horses—we feel compelled to make this absolutely clear.

We are convinced that whenever two or three gather together for the sake of management—in today's world—it's extremely easy to start thinking like bureaucrats. We need to recognize this tendency—laugh at it—and then run like crazed people back to sanity and common sense!

Dead Horse Strategy

The tribal wisdom of Dakota Indians, passed on from generation to generation, says that, when you discover that you are riding a dead horse, the best strategy is to dismount.

In our "modern world," however, a whole range of far more advanced strategies is often employed, such as:

- Buying a stronger whip
- Changing riders
- Threatening the horse with termination
- Appointing a committee to study the horse
- Arranging a visit to other countries to see how others ride a dead horse
- Lowering the standard so that dead horses can be included
- Hiring outside contractors to ride the dead horse
- Harnessing several dead horses together to increase the speed
- Providing additional funding and/or training to increase the dead horse's performance
- Doing a productivity study to see if lighter riders improve the dead horse's performance
- Saying things like, "This is the way we have always ridden this horse."
- Re-writing the expected performance requirements for all horses
- Promoting the dead horse to a supervisory position.

—Anonymous

God bless you, as you get serious about your job as leaders—and managers—of Christ's church. It's easy enough to weep and despair. Remember to keep on laughing! And tell yourself, "God is God—and I am not!"

About The Authors

Diane and Dell Shiell were married in 1973. They have been a team serving churches since 1978, the year Dell graduated from seminary and was ordained as a pastor.

They are passionate about the importance of intentional living and intentional ministry. They grew up in Minnesota, but have lived in Florida since 1990. They have three children and their spouses and six grandchildren, all of who live in Florida also. Dell served churches in Minnesota, Iowa, and Florida.

One of the highlights of their drive to be intentional was a year-long home and ministry exchange with a Norwegian pastor and his family in 1988-89. In 1990, they moved their family from Cedar Rapids, Iowa to serve a congregation in Nokomis, Florida. In 1991, while serving the congregation, they founded St. Hans Ministry Exchange, Inc., a non-profit Christian Home Exchange organization. In 1992, they published their first book, **Fair Exchange: A Ministry Exchange Between the USA and Norway.**

For several years, Diane worked in real estate. In 1995, Diane and Dell earned numerous designations, licenses, and certifications in financial services.

Dell became a CFP® professional, earning the Certified Financial Planner designation. Diane and Dell worked together as philanthropic estate planning consultants, then as church consultants.

In 2003, Diane and daughter, Megan Hess—both real estate brokers—founded a non-traditional real estate company, Venice Realty, Inc.

In 2016, Dell retired as a full-time parish pastor so he and Diane could spend more time with family, while continuing to encourage other Christians to discover the world of home exchanges. In 2016, they published their second book, **Go, Pastor, Go! (How clergy can take an affordable sabbatical that rejuvenates their soul, reunites their family, and reignites their congregation by using a home exchange.)** In 2016, they also published the second edition of their book, **Fair Exchange.**

In 2017, Dell served as an interim pastor; Dell and Diane spent a few months participating in the life of another congregation. This interim ministry experience accentuated a long-term awareness of the challenges facing struggling congregations these days. So many church leaders want to maintain a positive climate in their congregation, but it gets harder and harder to do so, given the realities of *an aging church* and *a shrinking church*.

The idea for their third book—**Can We Afford A Pastor?**—emerged. They decided to give churches a handle by which to critique their desire to have a full-time pastor relative to their church's financial position.

All three of their books are available (both print and Kindle editions) at Amazon.

Both Diane and Dell earned their bachelor degrees at the University of Minnesota. Dell earned his Master of Divinity and Doctor of Ministry at Luther Seminary, St. Paul, Minnesota.

To learn more about Diane and Dell's effort to promote home exchanges and give encouragement to pastors and congregations:

Visit ChristianHomeExchange.com today.

www.ingramcontent.com/pod-product-compliance
Lightning Source LLC
Chambersburg PA
CBHW061046110426
42740CB00049B/2480